The Life and Times

of

Peter Legh the Younger

(1707-1792)

A study of an Eighteenth Century Gentleman using the
correspondence of his Family, Friends and Associates

First published 1996 by
Geoff Simm, 19 Park Road North,
Newton-le-Willows, WA12 9TF

ISBN 0 9524787 1 4.

Design by Geoff Simm

Printed by Willow Printing
75/79 Back Cross Lane,
Newton-le-Willows,
Merseyside WA12 9YE
Tel. (0925) 222449 or 228524.

Foreword

Anyone who undertakes historical research soon finds themselves belonging to an eccentric fraternity who scuttle into record offices, pencil and notepad at the ready, intent on not wasting a single moment of precious opening time. At closing time we emerge, usually with the filth of the years on hands and clothes, sometimes triumphantly clutching a transcription of a vital piece of evidence it may have taken weeks to unearth. The joy of that find can only be shared with a fellow eccentric. In the depths of a record office I have been very tempted to yell "eureka!", I have heard the author of this book allow himself a mumbled "bingo!" But generally research work is a solitary occupation and one's enthusiasm has to be curbed for fear of being ejected on to the street.

For the past decade I have been privileged to share Geoff's delight as he transcribed the collection of letters on which he has based this work. The coffers of British Telecom must have gained considerably from the number of calls between our two homes. I have seen this book grow from a vague idea about an unknown man, dismissed as insignificant, virtually the only Legh since Tudor times not to have his portrait in the family home, to the biography it is now. At last Peter Legh the Younger has emerged, through his dusty letters, to take his rightful place in the long history of the Leghs of Lyme.

I hope that you, the reader, will enjoy the result of all those hours spent in Rylands Library and Cheshire Record Office. Research may sometimes be exceedingly tedious but, as in this case, it can sometimes be fascinating and very rewarding.

And, who knows, that missing portrait may just be in your attic!

Kate Atkinson.
Education Assistant for the National Trust at Lyme Park.

Acknowledgments

The author would like to thank the following people for their help in the production of this book: Kate Atkinson, Jean Coulthurst, Florence Wood, the Wroughton History Group, the staff at John Rylands University Library and the staff at Cheshire Record Office.

Permission to use the portrait of Martha Legh and the photograph of the marriage chair has been kindly given by the National Trust and Lord Newton.

Permission to use the Legh family letters in this publication has been kindly given by Lord Newton and the John Rylands University Library.

Front Cover - Lyme Park.
Back Cover - Martha Legh.
Background - Legh Family Letter.

Peter Legh the Younger

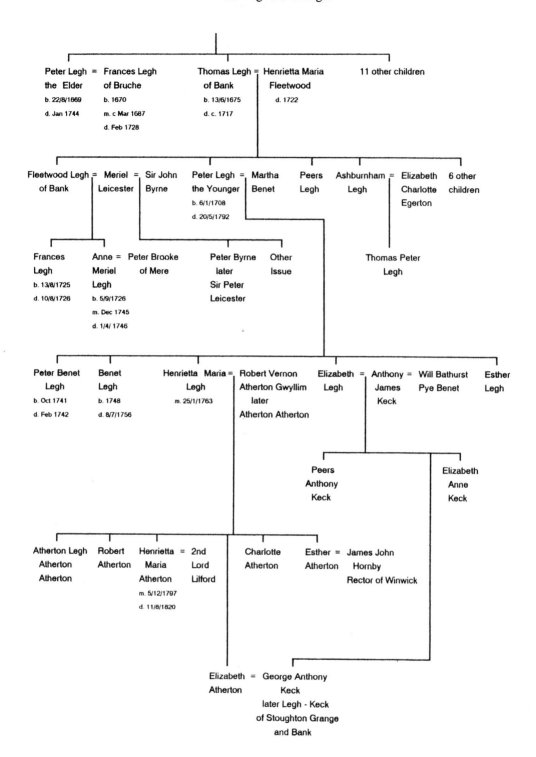

A section of the Legh Family Tree.

Introduction

The well known Cheshire family, the Leghs of Lyme, possesses a lineage that stretches back over 600 years of English history. They are intricately and repeatedly connected to many powerful and influential families in the country. Their family seat, Lyme Hall, situated at Disley in Cheshire, nestles in the foothills of the Pennines, its classical exterior giving an indication of the wealth of the family during the days of their occupancy.

On touring the lofty magnificent rooms many family portraits are found, men of power, knights, builders and movers of history. Their wives also appear, some beautiful, but mostly sad and hard, faces formed by a life of pain and sorrow.

Almost all members of the family are represented in some form or other, be it in portrait or sketch form. However, an intriguing omission is Peter Legh the Younger, seemingly forgotten amidst this impressive cavalcade of lordly Leghs. In the eighteenth century he was of some significance and power, being Lord of Lyme for nearly fifty years; a time that saw great changes nationally upon the industrial and social fronts, as well as on the Legh estates. Lady Newton, who chronicled the family's history in 'The House of Lyme' and 'Lyme Letters' summed up the period and the man in a few paragraphs, stating that Peter and his wife were unattractive and a 'dull and uninteresting couple'. His physical appearance is something of a mystery, because no portrait of him survives to the present day. A striking portrait of his wife, Martha, hangs in the Dining room at Lyme, giving an impression of certain regal qualities.

If Lyme Park is visited today, the guides admit to "skipping over" the eighteenth century section of the family history, claiming that it is rather bland and uninteresting. However, although Peter's time at Lyme cannot be classed as glamourous, with knights, battles and severed arms, it was still an essential part of the family and its history. The involvement with trade and the part that he played in the industrial revolution that was sweeping the country are just a few points that must in some way be recorded and acknowledged.

Therefore, it may be asked, who was Peter Legh the Younger, who ruled the Legh estates two hundred years ago?

Bank Hall, Bretherton.

Birth

Peter Legh the Younger was born on the 7th January 1707, in Lancashire at Bank Hall in Bretherton. He was christened a few miles away at Aughton, a small village south of Ormskirk. In today's reckoning Peter would have been born in 1708. His birth was recorded as being in 1707 because at that time the beginning of the year was on the 25th of March. The start of a new year was only changed to the 1st of January in 1752.

Peter's birth was to herald a new era in the fortunes of the Legh family of Lyme Hall. The fortuitous ownership of the Haydock estate in Lancashire was to come to fruition in a dramatic way. Over the forthcoming century the Leghs were able to take advantage of the large amounts of coal beneath the township to fuel the industrial revolution. The ensuing revenue enabled the Leghs to live in luxury and style throughout the eighteenth century, and laid the foundation for the future expansion of their estates.

However, during the first part of his life, it was thought that he would take little part in that venture, because he was only a minor nephew with, to all appearances, a healthy elder brother. His father, Thomas Legh, was the younger brother of the then Lord of Lyme, Peter Legh the Elder. Throughout his life, Thomas Legh had been an active member of parliament for Newton, being returned in 1698, 1701, 1702, 1705, 1708 and 1710. He had married, in 1701, Henrietta Maria, the daughter and heiress of Sir Thomas Fleetwood of Bank Hall, Bretherton. After the death of Henrietta's father, the couple lived at Bank Hall and between 1702 and 1715 had 10 children. As a long serving MP, Thomas spent long periods residing in London. He was forced, probably due to lack of funds, into sharing accommodation with his mother, in Devonshire St. Soho, upon, to all accounts, unfriendly terms.

The latter part of Thomas Legh's life is somewhat veiled in mystery. He died about 1717, possibly in London, and it is likely that he left his wife and children with little money, having only the Bank Hall estate to support them. Of the children, four of the boys survived to adulthood: Fleetwood, Peter, Peers and Ashburnham; a fact that became very important in the ensuing years. Their mother, Henrietta Maria Legh, died in 1722 and the remaining children were taken into the care and protection of their uncle, Peter Legh the Elder. A letter from the eldest son, Fleetwood, in 1722, thanked his uncle for his kind gesture:-

"I am very sensible that upon the death of my dear Mother the affairs of our Family are in so great confusion that I have not knowledge or Ability to undertake them and am very much obliged to You for the Kind offer of Your Advice and Instruction in Your letter to my Uncle. I earnestly beg that You will take me, my Brs and Sisters into your Protection and be so good as to Manage our Affairs which we are So unable to do ourselves."

This letter was written with a certain amount of anguish on the part of young Fleetwood. The death of his mother, poor advice and wayward ways had left him somewhat in debt. Although he was heir to the Bank Hall estate, the financial position still left his younger brothers and sisters unprovided for. It was Peter Legh the Elder's generosity and business sense that was to save Fleetwood's family from ruin and poverty. He instructed his solicitor to set up a trust, using sections of the Bank Hall estate as collateral, to provide money for the younger children. Fleetwood's sisters were to receive £600 each at the age of 21 and his brothers £500 each. Also £140 per annum was to be raised to provide for their upkeep. All these arrangements were linked with the impending marriage of Fleetwood Legh.

Home

Bank Hall, Peter's first family home, belonged to his mother's family and so became part of his father's estate on their marriage. After his mother, Henrietta Maria, died it was passed down to Fleetwood Legh in 1722. In 1726, he in turn left the estate to his daughter, Ann Meriel Legh, who married in 1745 Peter Brooke the Younger. In April 1746 she died without issue and under the age of 21, whereupon the estate reverted back to Peter Legh the Younger, he being the next in line to Fleetwood Legh. In Peter Legh's will, dated 1787, the Bank Hall estate was grouped with other minor estates to be sold or rented to provide money for his daughters. Afterwards, when it was no longer required for that purpose, it was left to his grandson, George Anthony Keck. The only proviso was that he had to assume and use the surname Legh, hence his name became George Anthony Legh Keck. However, he only gained control of the estate after an appeal against an added codicil in Peter's will. During the time of his ownership the original Jacobean mansion was greatly extended, with many of the extensions being embellished with the Ram's Head. Bank Hall stayed in his hands until his death, then, because he had no issue, passed to the children of his cousin, Henrietta Maria Atherton, who had married, in 1797, the Rt. Hon. Thomas Powys, second Baron Lilford. From then onwards it formed part of the Lilford estates, as it still does today. In this century the building was used as a private residence and then by the local council until the 1970s, but due to extensive dry rot and political wrangling it has fallen into a state beyond any economical repair.

Today, Bank Hall stands in a sea of tall grass and is extensively covered by creepers and overgrown trees, reminiscent of a modern day sleeping beauty's castle. The tower is broken and sections of the facade are strewn throughout the grounds. Inside, the upper floors have fallen through and lie in great heaps in the ground floor rooms, with the massive floor beams embedded in the piles of rubbish -- a sad end to a fine building.

𝔉leetwood

By the 1720s it was realised by Peter Legh the Elder that he would father no male heir and he therefore decided to settle his estates upon his four nephews. The eldest, Fleetwood, was to inherit all of the estate after the death of his uncle, in consideration of an intended marriage to Meriel Leicester, the daughter of Sir Francis Leicester of Tabley Hall in Cheshire. Peter Legh the Elder was very pleased with the match, being a close friend and prolific correspondent of Sir Francis. After their marriage, Fleetwood and Meriel Legh took up residence at Bank Hall. They appear, from their correspondence, to have had little money, with a number of persistent debts. A little assistance was given by Peter Legh the Elder and Sir Francis, but the overall impression was that they hoped the young couple could manage their own affairs. There is evidence that Fleetwood carried a series of debts for a number of years. In 1724 they were listed and amounted to £2669. By June 1725 he was still in debt to the sum of £1447. Some of that debt came from before his marriage, when he was attracted by London's high life. His tutor Robert Shippen, referred to it in 1722:-

"Mr Fleetwoods Conduct has not been so unblameable as I could wish and I am unwilling to complain when there are hopes and promises of amendments. Young men will be guilty of some follies and they must be overlookt sometimes. I have no other reason to be much concerned for the Death of his Mother but that it may lead him into an Imagination that he has an Estate fallen into his hands. I will endeavour to undeceive him in that particular; but in my opinion it would be more effectually done by You if you would give him leave to wait upon You for a month or two at Lyme."

Robert Shippen was concerned that Fleetwood was getting into bad ways and wanted Peter Legh the Elder to back him up in encouraging Fleetwood to become more responsible.

Fleetwood referred to money many times in letters to his father-in-law. These extracts indicate his concern:-

"I thought myself very happy from the first, and much honoured, in being accepted by You for a son and, Your Daughter for a Husband, and it is with great pleasure; I assure you that happiness daily improves, and the goodness with which my wife receives my constant study to oblige, makes me hope it is in some measure acceptable to her, which consideration (as well as gratitude) will make me persevere, and use her as so much Innocence, and so much goodness deserves; and if a strict obedience to all your commands will place me in that rank of esteem with you, which I very much covet (and only wish to merit) I shall be perfectly happy."

"I heartily thank you for the kind offer of Your Coach horses, and shall be very fond of them, both as they came from You, and as they are valuable in themselves. I desire leave for to say I am surprised You should think; I expected a present of a new Coach, I am already too much Indebted to ask for more, and all I meant was that You would bespeak me one and I will very gladly allow You what it comes to out of the interest money from Ireland."

"as to the £1000 You were so kind to give us to set up with, I can assure You I am to sensible of the advantage and kindness of the present to have it signify nothing however it is blunged in the articles"

"I know myself to be perfectly happy in haveing such an Uncle and such a Father. I will observe Your kind caution, in paying all my just debts, and not being bound, lest as You rightly observe I cancel the obligation."

"I think myself entirely happy in a wife and am resolved (with Gods blessing) to live so as neither she nor my circumstances shall be uneasy, I heartily thank you for Your kind advice."

From this correspondence it is obvious that Fleetwood had to be very careful regarding his father-in-law. Sir Francis Leicester was a powerful man in the country and would have no disobedience from minor relatives. Besides the obvious problems with money, the letters also show the depth of feeling for his wife.

After their marriage, Peter Legh the Elder lived in hopes of the young couple producing a son. In a letter written in 1724 he made the comment:-

"heartily praying that a Blessing may attend the young Couple."

Unfortunately, from Peter Legh's point of view, Fleetwood and Meriel were only blessed with two daughters, one born before and one after Fleetwood's death. Sadly the first child died an infant, but the second, Ann Meriel, survived and later married Peter Brooke the Younger.

The sudden death of Fleetwood Legh in January 1726 threw all the family plans into disarray. It was first mentioned in a letter from Peter Legh the Elder to Sir Francis Leicester on the 23rd of that month:-

"I had writt a letter to you the last post, but was so surprized with a messenger from Bank, that brought me the Mellancholly account of My Nephew Leghs death and am so senciable of My Neice Leghs Condition I could not tell what to say to you, nor am I now much better, only am resolved to write in hopes of an Amendment, after I have told you that my heavy heart dos condole with you."

He again wrote a week later with more news:-

"I am favoured with your Letter and at this troublesome time, I must beg your directions, for raily, I cannot tell how to advise the Family at Bank, I would rather serve them direct. I have sent to Bank with a how do and expect the bearer tomorrow. Just now I have received a letter from Mr Gorse, that he designes to be with me next Saturday and so to go from me to Bank. I will let him know what I have told you and hope I shall hear from you, by the return of this post, and pray direct your letter to me at Haydock Lodge."

These letters indicate how shocked and saddened Peter Legh was at his nephew's early death. All his plans for the future had been dashed. Meanwhile, Meriel had written to her father with her sad news:-

"My dear Papa,
God knows I am in great Grief
for poor Mr Legh: who was a most kind husband, I pray God grant you
your life: and my poor little dear Baby's and of most humbly desire your
Blessing and prayers for poor me and little one who is ill of a cold which
adds still to my Grief: but I beseech God to enable me to bear it as I
ought."

The sad events of 1726 changed the history of the Legh family completely. Peter Legh the Younger became the heir apparent at the age of 19. The correspondence seems to indicate that he accepted it with mixed feelings. His schooling was not yet complete and his uncle would have to begin again with his search for a suitable bride for one of his nephews.

Hon'd Sr.   Stockp:t Dec:r ij:th 1726.

Inclosed are a few papers, wch will Shew if
how my Brother and I have Spent a part
of our time this year: We break up School
on friday and Shall be glad to wait on if
will out good frind, when ever if please to
send for my Brother and

Sr

if obed.t duty.l nephew

P: Legh.

Peter's handwriting as a boy.

16

Education

The early education of Peter Legh the Younger would have been taken at home, probably with private tutor.   Various comments in the family correspondence indicate that he was a shy, reticent child of diminutive size and that not much was expected of him.   However, all that was to change when he entered Westminster School in London.   It was to be the making of him.   His feelings are described in a letter to his uncle:-

"I being now att home My Mother ordered Me to write to You, and the first opportunity I could possible get was no little joy to Me, To think that I had sutch a good opportunity of performing My Duty and My Desire is to lett You know how I like Westminster School, And that I like My Boarding exceedingly well, Especially Westminster School which is My Daily Delight, and particulary the promiss which I made in Making My Study My daily Delight, Pray give My Duty To My Aunt."

About that time, Robert Shippen, principal of Brasenose College, Oxford, made several comments about Peter in his letters to Peter Legh the Elder:-

"Mr Peter was with me this Christmas and I think he improves very much and will answer the expectations of his friends."

In another letter he says:-

"Little Pee behaves himself very well and beyond all expectation and I do not doubt Westminster Pee's success."

At the time of these letters Peter was in his teens and his brother Fleetwood was still alive.   Little did they realise that in the near future "Little Pee" was to be the heir apparent and the future power on the estates.

Whenever Peter Legh the Elder stayed in London his nephew, young Peter, would visit him from school.   The two became friendly and

Peter Legh the Younger assisted his uncle with his correspondence if ever he was ill. Peter Legh the Elder's feelings for his nephew appeared in a letter in 1723:-

"My other nephew Peter, hee's with me during the Play dayes. I like him very well and he has a good character."

When this was written, Peter Legh the Elder was staying two houses from Russell House, the London home of Sir Francis Leicester. This is an example of Young Peter helping his uncle with a reply:-

"My uncle Legh being confined to His room and unable to write obliges me to answer the favour of yours ---- I returned to Lyme out of Wiltshire on Friday last, and hope all things are in a fair way to be well. For these two last days My Uncle Legh has gained strength, tho as yet quite unable to stand; My Uncle Captain is got out of his Room again."

The Captain referred to was Richard Legh (1679-1742); he had been in the Horse Guards and some letters tell of him having a drink problem. The amusing remark inferred that he was sometimes locked away, probably during a drinking bout.

By 1727 pressure was being applied to Peter Legh the Younger to make a decision about his career. He had not yet settled on a university college and repeatedly sought his uncle's advice with regard to both those points. His uncle's dilemma is evident in a series of letters written in 1727, beginning in April:-

"I take freedom to trouble you with the enclosed, it is from My nephew P:L: and the great Matter now in hand is whether he should go into Orders, or not, You can see he leaves it to me, I am loath to direct, unless I was Master of his inclinations and qualifications. Therefore I have writt to him to lay his hand upon his heart and do as he pleases, I will assist him the best I can. I do acknowledge that I have received a good Character of him, but there is so much depending upon the behaviour of a Divine, that I owne I sho'ld be glad to see him a deserving one, on the other hand it would be always be a trouble to see him otherwayes. At

present the chief thing is, whether Cambridge or Oxford, Brazenose is laid aside."

After Sir Francis' reply Peter again wrote:-

"Your Letter I'll burn as desired, it confirms me in my opinion, and yet I have lately made an Enquiry from another hand that gives Christ Church the same Character as the other College has, so that I'me at present inclined to persuade my Nep: to stay where he is for another year. What startles me the most is the thoughts of him studying the Law, there might have been some hopes if he had been put onto an Attorney."

By the end of May young Peter seemed obsessed with the idea of Brazenose College:-

"I have just now received Your Letter of the 20th and the one before that, and as you were pleased to Advise about My Nep: P:L: I agreed with him yesterday, to stay another year with Doctr Fr(ederick) but found him absolutely sett upon Brazenose if he had now left Westminster, not so much upon the qualifications of that College, as to some reflections throwne upon the other two."

Indecision still reigned a week later:-

"My Nephew P:L: hee's still with me and when he returns, he will either go to Westminster again or go to My Mothers in order to get some Masters to qualify him in the Mathematicks, Dancing and such like -- which is to divert him, or else Brazenose runs in his head, I owne I can't imagin the reason of it."

In this letter Peter Legh the Elder sounds as if he was reaching the end of his tether. However, all was settled by October. Young Peter entered St John's College at Cambridge. His uncle wrote with the good news to Sir Francis:-

"I have been tedious in not writing, but raily, I deferred it, untill I had sent my Nep: P:L: to Cambridge, the

*servant and Parson Downes return'd last night left him well, and well
pleased with Doct: Newcome his Tutor and the Doctor the same with him
passed his examination to satisfaction, so I hope with Gods blessing he
will do."*

The last remark by Peter Legh the Elder was obviously made with
a certain amount of relief.

Young Peter's meek manner sometimes appeared when he came
into contact with Sir Francis Leicester, who must have been quite a fierce
character. The next letter describes a cosy but serious chat between the
two Peters:-

*"I received both your Letters (I thank you
for them) in the former you desired to kno: something of what you and I
were talking of concerning my nephew. The other evening no one but
him and I together I asked him how long he designed staying in the
Country, he say'd to the Middle of October, what sayes I don't you
designe waiting upon Sir F:L: Yes when you please, but raily say's he, I
have always a concern upon me, that makes me uneasy in his company,
he ask's so many Questions I'me afraid of him, Why then says I ask him
questions again, the more free you are with him, I'me sure you will be
more welcome, for he has a kindness for you, Ay says he, I believe too, he
smiled and some body coming in put a stop to us, but by this you may be
assured that there is nothing at all of what you were apprehensive off
which with pleasure I say it."*

Peter Legh the Younger would have been at college until after
1731. Ahead of him lay the search for a suitable bride and the heady
responsibilty of his inheritance.

Marriage

During the early 1730s, Peter Legh the Elder cast his net far and wide to gain a suitable bride for his nephew, Peter Legh the Younger. He studied reports of various eligible young ladies of good background and requested information from many of his friends about suitability, appearance, money and family connections. However, there is a distinct possibility that young Peter's marriage wasn't an arranged one at all, but a love match. The future in-laws of young Peter, the Benets of Salthrop, Wiltshire, owned or rented a house in Gay Street, Bath, probably using it during the summer season. Peter Legh the Younger, an obsessive visitor to Bath throughout his adult life, could have met and courted Martha Benet during his visits to the spa and the inevitable evening parties. Bath at that time was known for its social life as well as the medicinal waters, being the 'in' place to visit.

The marriage agreement, dated 6th January 1737, was an updated version of the 1723 agreement. Martha was allowed £10,000 to dispose of in her Will and, very cleverly, she insisted on allowances of £100 per annum until the death of Peter Legh the Elder and then £200 per annum for the rest of her life, *'for her own perculiar expences and wearing apparel'*.

Peter Legh and Martha Benet took their marriage vows twice, satisfying both families and friends at Lyme and Salthrop. They were married at St Mary's, Disley on the 20th December 1737 and at Wroughton Church on the 7th January 1738.

Peter Legh the Elder graciously welcomed Martha into his family in the following manner:-

> *"Madam,*
> *I am but an indifferent writer at the best*
> *yet I cannot forbear sending you my best Congratulations on the late*
> *Allyance into My Family, being confirmed by my nephew Leghs Letter*
> *this day received.*
> *Madam I do assure you, I can't repress the*
> *pleasure I have from all hands of your great and Good Character,*
> *especially at this Time, that I must desire to be esteemed as I am in*

Martha Legh, wife of Peter Legh the Younger.

reality, your well wisher and Madam Your Most Affectionate Uncle and humble servant."

During the first years of their married life the young couple lived at Calveley Hall, Cheshire. It was a small estate left to the Legh family in the will of Sir Hugh Calveley of Lea. Peter and Martha spent an idyllic interlude at Calveley with none of the future problems and responsibilities that were to come their way.

One of a pair of chairs made for Peter & Martha Legh on their marriage.

Uncle

By the 1740s, old age and ill health had begun to take its toll upon Peter Legh the Elder. He had reached the age of 75 and had outlived most of his family and friends. During the latter years of his life his nephews, Peter and Peers, assisted him greatly with the running of the estates. Various references to his many disorders began to appear in the correspondence throughout the early 1740s. These are a selection written by Peers in 1743:-

"Doctr. Nichoson was here this day, I desired him to see my Uncle, find the disorder in his head, as I have mention in my Last, to turn out the Gout, one of his feet being swel'd, Likewise a touch in his hand it has reduc'd him very much, he's very low spirit'd -- his stomack has fail'd him for some days past -- so leave the rest to your Judgment."

"I think my Uncle is something Easier, then when I (writ) last, his Cheife Complaint is in his head, neither is his Stomach so good, which is a sad symtom."

"Our old Gentleman is a good deal Wors - then when I writ you last, for four or five days last past has been very dul, not so good Stomack, Yesterday he was Sick at his Dinner, Complain'd of Pain in his head. Will, Bath'd his head with Brandy, I thought made him Easier; In my Opinion he cannot hold it long. with the bad nights he has."

Peers was correct with his last remark because Peter Legh the Elder only survived another 3 months to January of the following year. He was interred at St. Oswald's, Winwick, in an unmarked grave, as was his wish. Peter Legh the Younger was now Lord of Lyme and he probably took up residence there immediately.

𝔚𝔦𝔣𝔢

Martha Legh, the wife of Peter Legh the Younger, was the only daughter of Thomas Benet of Salthrop, Wiltshire. Her family had lived and farmed the Salthrop estate since the middle of the previous century and had become reasonably wealthy in the process. Thomas Benet communicated with Peter Legh and Martha several times during the early 1740s. His letters were full of information on 18th century social graces and society life, with chit chat about various debts and the standing of certain individuals. This is a typical example written in June 1743:-

*"As it is always a pleasure to hear from Calveley; so both you and my
Daughter are very kind in giving us that opportunity by yours Which I
wrote some little time since, and my Daughter's -- which arrived here last
post, for both which I am very thankfull. I am also oblig'd by your so
ready a Compliance with what my Nephew Benet Garrard wrote to you
relating to the one months interest money, and it is no small satisfaction
to me that I have liv'd to discharge that debt as agreed on, being desirous
to be as punctual as possible in the performance of everything stipulated
on my part. The loss of Mr Wm. Shippen as you mention is a publick one,
and as you have thoughts of being in the house, I think you judge right in
taking the opportunity of succeeding him, where I presume you are in no
danger of an opposition, nor of creating much expence. We have just
rec'd an Account of the death of your late friend Mr John Egerton's
Daughter of Tatton, whereby I suppose that estate is eas'd of ten thousand
pounds debt, the present owner of which seems to be a very good sort of a
man, as indeed do all the family a people we are very glad to hear that
you are got so well, which we hope will continue and that my Daughter
enjoys so good health."*

Peter Legh the Younger eventually took his father-in-law's advice and was first returned as MP for Newton in 1747.

Throughout the early years of their marriage Martha and Peter were very close. After the birth of their children, Martha accompanied Peter wherever he went whether it was to London, during parliamentary sessions, or to Bath in the spa season. A letter written early in their marriage showed the depth of feeling for her husband:-

Salthrop House, Wiltshire.

"My Dear Dear Love,"
"I can't forbear scribbling 2 or 3 lines by
Peers who we found at Calvely last night when we came home from
Chester; we drank Tea at Mrs Owen's; who enquired after thee and sent
all their saarvices; G. Parry came in while we were there and looks
exceeding ghastly and nastily indeed: he told me Nat. Booth was married
to Miss Jones; and that Mrs. Gibbons had made her worth £15,000;
whether Mrs. Gibbons is dead or not I don't know, but I can easily believe
she'll give her that in the whole. We would've persuaded Peers to've
stay'd with us another day, but as he'd given his word to be at Lyme
tomorrow night, we wouldn't press it, lest he should quite lose his credit.
I hope thou'st been quite well my Dear Rogue since thou left us, and that
we shall see thee Thursday or Friday even at farthest. I sent on Saturday
to Hammer's, and poor Shonny was got there so soon, that I doubt he did
not meet with an agreeable reception at home. The Eaton Family is all
well, where I spen on Sunday. Betty Dod din'd here today on her way
thither, she's indeed much out of order (of) a kind of an Asthma and
designs to have advice at Chester for it, together with the same for her
£500 as we suppose; for Brooks of Mere writes her word he can't justise
to the Merediths, the paying her the money, but she thinks that as she's
had interest pay'd, 'tis a sufficient acknowledgement: of the justice of the
debt. Prythee come to us again as soon as possible; I shall hope for
Thursday evening. Adieu My Dearest Dearest Rogue, I am for ever and
ever Thy Pat."

This is obviously a letter straight from the heart, full of affection and gossip about friends and acquaintances.

As time passed however, things did not go too well. The death of their son and the further disappointment of not producing another heir caused a rift between the couple. Martha also became more independent and gained control of a separate income, other than that from her husband. Richard Orford, the steward, kept her accounts but they were separate from the rest of the family. Her letters to Richard Orford tell of various deals and transactions of her own and of her, as early as 1767, travelling around the country alone. Here she was giving orders about her return to Lyme:-

*"I intend setting off from this place tomorrow sennight, and shall lay at
Bakewell on Tuesday night, so send the 4 Chaise horses and a saddle
horse for Harry early on wensday morning that I may be at home by
Dinner at 3 oclock or soon after, Pray tell Patty that she may get the
Rooms ready."*

Another problem that began to appear in Martha's life was the increasing friction with her sister-in-law, Ann. By the latter part of her marriage she was not in control of her own home, she always had to defer to Ann in most matters. The friction between the two women, plus the appearance of another woman in local gossip, culminated in the dramatic letter of July, 1783 :-

"Mr Legh,"
*The uncomfortable life you must needs be sensible I have led in your
Family and the sort of behaviour I have met with there for these many
years past gives me every room to think that my absence will be by much
the most agreeable to every part of it I therefore purpose to continue in
this part of the World some length of time longer for I wish to spend the
latter part of these my days with peace and comfort. I think it but right I
should acquaint you with this intention.*
I am yrs very affectionately
Mar. Legh"

This letter is full of bitterness about the conduct of people at Lyme and indicated that she had had enough and had decided to live apart from her husband. Dealings between Peter and Martha were organised through a go-beween, Thomas Davenport, the MP for Newton. In a letter from Thomas Davenport, dated August 1783, Martha is making sure that she has money for the future, by selling her Salthrop property:-

*"A letter from Mrs. Legh informes me, that she agrees to the Terms
proposed, viz giving up the whole Salthrop property, & taking 600£ per
ann. to herself, and 166£ 13s 4d to Miss Legh."*

It must have been with great regret that she was forced to give up her family property. A footnote to a following letter shows her feelings regarding that point:-

"I forgot to mention that Mrs. Legh wishes to know if she may have the liberty of coming at times to the Salthrop House, when you take possession of the Estate."

A few years were to pass before any contact was made between the estranged parties, albeit a tentative one, with the underlyng disagreements still evident:-

"Mrs Keck having given me a Note of the China that is wanted at Lyme and Haydock, I must say I do not like to undertake buying it unless I had Orders from the higher Powers; well knowing that what I do, cannot give the satisfaction of those that are more in favor, and whose performances are more approv'd. Therefore till I have directions thro' you, I shall desist meddling in the matter."

She obviously wrote this letter with a certain amount of sarcasm regarding her persecutors at Lyme. The term "higher powers" most certainly referred to Ann Legh.

The earlier reference to "another woman" came from a rather cruel cartoon that appeared in 1779:-

"Peter L--- Esqr L-me.

A house divided against itself.

Except the Painter's happiness in maintaining a striking family likeness under the impressions of very different sensations, we cannot say this performance does him credit. The principal is the only figure who essentially differs from the others in point of dress, his white smug periwig makes his ruddy complexion a good caricature of a body coachman.
The attention he pays to a female, whose countenance is the picture of envy, is as disgusting as her attitude is

mysterious, for she is leading him, like a blind man, with the right hand, from his Lady and two Daughters, and supporting with the left another daughter quite overburdened with the heaviness of her drapery. The wrinkles of his Lady's face are the melancholy furrows of excessive grief. The two Daughters next to the disconsolate mother regard her with most dutiful respect. The countenance of the elder sister is replete with Virtue, Sensibility and the most placid Temper; this appears to be more the effect of situation than any studied intention of the Artist to make her more comfortable."

The people referred to in the skit were listed at the end of the work:-

> Mrs Ath--ton (eldest daughter)
> Mrs Legh of Lyme
> Miss Legh of Lyme
> Mrs Ann Legh (sister of Peter)
> Lady Mary W-st (the designing female)

At the time of the cartoon, Peter was then 72, so if the accusations were true, he must have been active for his age, but the correspondence infers the opposite to be true. However, a Lady Mary West did exist about that time, she was the eldest daughter of Henry, fourth Earl of Stamford. In 1779, she would have been approximately 40, a good age for a designing female!

Martha's Will, dated 1st October 1784, bequeathed the majority of her money and possessions to her daughter, Hester, other than small gifts to friends and 5 guineas each to her Nan and maid servants. Throughout the document there is not one mention of her estranged husband, Peter.

Towards the end, Peter and Martha's marriage had become a formal one, in name only. Contemporary references about Martha indicate that she was an intelligent, independent woman, with a pleasant personality. The striking portrait of her, in the Dining room at Lyme, shows her to be a typical lady of the day. Martha Legh returned to Lyme, where she died on the 21st June 1787. However it must have been her last wish to be buried in Wiltshire, because her body was taken from Lyme and buried in Wroughton Church, near to her family estate.

Children

     Peter and Martha Legh had five children, two boys and three girls. The story of the two boys is a sad one, neither of them reached adulthood. Peter Benet, the eldest, was born at Calveley in October, 1741 and was christened at the local church. Peter wrote with the good news to Sir Francis Leicester:-

"Be pleas'd to accept at My most humble thanks for the favour of your very obliging Epistle, And when I consider how much I'm almost asham'd to aske further favours: My Brother (the bearer of this) being called to Oxford obliges Us to Baptise the Child the 20th of this Month which is sooner than we propos'd, And if you'l be so good to stand Godfather with Mr Benet the obligation shall ever be acknowledged."

     He also informed his uncle Peter of the happy event:-

"A great many thanks is due to you for your very Obliging Epistle, We have this day made a Xristian of our Babe by the name of Peter Benet Legh, Pe Warburton Represented Sr Frances, myself for My Father Benet, and Nancy for Sister Holt, Your present of Venison was very acceptable, And if one May judge by (that) companies eating was very good."

     However, all was not well with the child. The church records for All Saints, Handley, relate the sad tale :-

"Peter Bennet Leigh son of Peter Leigh Esq of Calveley bapt October 1741."

     And just a few lines later:-

"Peter Bennet Leigh son of Peter Leigh Esq from Chester Buried February 24 1742."

The second of the boys, Benet, was born in 1748 at Lyme. He was christened at St Mary's, Disley, on the 1st October of that year. Benet Legh, being heir to the estates, must have been the apple of his father's eye and Peter continually requested news of his progress during his trips away from home. Lady Newton refers to the portrait of the golden child at Lyme and Peter must have thought that he and his wife had succeeded in producing a healthy heir. In the late 1740s and early 1750s all was beautiful in the life of Peter and Martha Legh. John Worthington, the Steward, reported to Peter the delightful goings on at Lyme:-

"Dear Misses Legh are both very well and continue as merry as can be, and I'me become so great a favourite with Miss Hen. that I have frequent Visits from her, and when at Dinner she'l come to my knee, and all that hear her pritty and witty conversation which makes all merry. Upon the delivery of your kind kiss to Miss Hen. I was comanded by her to return'd to her Papa and Mamma her Duty and thanks and to let you both know that both She and her sister Betty (as she calls her) were very well."

And again in 1747:-

"As soon as Miss Hen. was told Letters were come on this morning from her Pappa, she desired to come down to my Office to enquire after her Pappa and Mamma's welfare, wherefore Mrs Kennion brought both my little Jewels to me, who on your behalf I received and embraced most Tenderly, they are both quite hearty and well. & Miss Hen. says she dare venture to Ride behind me, & I may carry She says Miss Betty before me, as far as Old Rachels to meet and welcome her Pappa and Mamma home."

In a letter dated 27th March 1748, John Worthington gave Henrietta some news:-

"I took my little Jewels to deliver 'em Your kind kisses, and gave Miss Hen. your hints that She had a sister Coming, but she look earnest at Me and said No, No, what then Miss Hen. said I would you rather Choose a Bro' No, No, says she not yet, not yet."

Peter Legh loved to reply to John Worthington's letters, requesting ever more news of his children. Below are two letters from 1752 about his special joy, Benet:-

"I had the satisfaction of Yrs this morning and am made sufficiently happy in the very Good Account you give of our Dear little Jewels, the little Mans Request of New Cloaths was well paid for in the Horn Pipe, and as you Observe to him The peer he makes will his New cloaths the sooner he'l demand New ones again."

"Its the Utmost happiness to Me to hear such frequent Good Accounts of our Dear little Nursery, And I do desire the little Horn Piper And his Sisters may dance you out of all their little Demands, And its not the least satisfaction to Me that the time draws near When I shall be a jovial Eye witness of their little Exploits."

The couple, however, were dealt a crushing blow in 1756, when little Benet died at the age of 7. It was a blow that was to damage their marriage as well as causing much grief. A large elaborate memorial was erected in the Legh chapel at Winwick church, with a very sad and heartfelt inscription:-

"Flebilis Ille Nulli Flebilior Quam Patri Aflictissimo"

The translation is:-

"He was mourned, but by none more bitterly than his much afflicted father"

However more success can be related with the three girls. They all grew to be healthy and intelligent young ladies, two of them marrying well. The eldest, Henrietta Maria, was married in 1763 to Robert Vernon Atherton Gwyllim of Atherton and Bewsey. Robert Gwyllim was an extensive landowner and speculator in the locality. He later changed his name becoming Robert Vernon Atherton Atherton, strengthening his connections with the local district. Their eldest daughter, Henrietta Maria

Interr'd in the Vault beneath, lies the
Remains of MASTER BENET LEGH,
only Son of *Peter Legh Esq.* of Lyme,
in the County Palatine of Chester, by
Madam Martha Legh, only Daughter of
Tho.ˢ Benet Esq. of Salthrop, in the
County of Wilts.
He died the 8ᵗʰ of July, 1755.
Aged 8 Years.

Memorial to Benet Legh in the
Legh Chapel at St. Oswald's, Winwick.

Atherton, married Thomas Powys, who became Lord Lilford in 1792. On her marriage Henrietta Maria was a wealthy heiress, owning estates in Atherton, Pennington, Bewsey, Burtonwood, Sankey and Penketh. Their second daughter, Elizabeth Atherton, married her first cousin, George Anthony Keck, who later changed his name to Legh Keck to gain control of his inheritance from Peter Legh's Will.

Elizabeth Legh, the second daughter of Peter Legh the Younger, married Anthony James Keck of Stoughton Grange, near Leicester. The Kecks were quite a wealthy family and Anthony would have been a good catch for Elizabeth. He became very popular with his father-in-law because, later, Anthony gave up his parliamentary seat at Stoughton and took the position at Newton. This is a letter from him to Peter Legh in 1764, showing his love for Elizabeth:-

"I am most friendly & sincerely concerned at this violent return of your Cholick; & much more so as I am afraid your regard for me has in a great measure aggravated your Complaint - My late unpardonable Crime shall be the last; & I hope that only indiscretion (but that is too gentle a name) you can ever attribute to me. Your friendship & confidence make me appear (if possible) more criminal; which join'd with the perfection & beauty of your Daughter render me the most unhappy man existing - A(nne) gives me great encouragement; & I hope to be able in about a week or rather sooner; to make one of the most aggreeable; i think I may with propriety add the most united family I ever lived in. My life & happiness depends upon yourself, Miss Anne, & My Dear Miss Legh; who I really have so great a regard for; that I would submit to a voluntary Banishment; sooner than she should be that best sufferer by my indiscretion or weakness & inconsistency."

Some intriguing questions arise from the above remarks; had Anthony been indiscreet with another woman, or was he just over zealous in his wooing of his future bride?

Their son, George Anthony Keck, must have been a particular favourite of his grandfather, Peter, because he was specifically referred to in his will, regarding the Brotherton estate.

All three daughters of Peter and Martha received a good education. Below is a letter of Hester Legh, written in French to her mother, probably from school:-

"My Very Dear Mother,
It is with all the pleasure in the world that I write to you, I hope soon to
have a letter from my father because I have great pleasure in receiving
his news, I beg you to escuse the faults that you notice in this letter which
is the second which I have sent to you, I ask you to make my respects to
my father my aunt and my best wishes to my sister and my brother, I am,
My very dear Mother your obedient daughter, Hester Legh."

The next letter is by Elizabeth Keck, written to her mother from London where she was probably staying because of her husband's parliamentary duties. Her thoughts are full of children, her own and her sister's:-

"My dear Mamma may be surprized to see my handwriting but
could not help wishing her Joy of My Sister Hennys increase of family,
which I find will be in a few months, I rejoice at it as I'm sure Sisters
great desire of a little family; and I'm sure she'l find great pleasure in
them, thank God both mine are very well, and I think I can say, (without
the least partiallity) they are two of the finest boys that was seen, nay:
forgive me if I say they are handsome, Princess Louisa Ann, always
speaks to them when she meets them in Kensington Gardens. I am glad to
find Miss Gwillym married so well, in general its thought a very good
match for her. I'm sorry to hear you have been ill but its what every body
here complains of; a very cold and fever, my two dear little boys have
been ill, but with a little nursing thank God are gott very well again,
Anthony has gott no teeth, and Peers only poor one, and that he has had
from a month old, we are just going out to supper, therefore conclude
with being

Dear Mamma
Your Dutiful Daughter,
E: Keck.
PS pray my love to my Sister Hetty."

Peter Legh's concern over his daughters' future financial position appeared in his will. He insisted in making extra payments to ensure that they were provided for for the foreseeable future. Having no male issue to carry on his name, Peter was forced, with much regret, to pass his estates to his nephew, Thomas Peter Legh.

𝔅rothers

Throughout his life Peter Legh seemed to have been on friendly terms with his brothers, Fleetwood, Peers and Ashburnham. When Peter was a teenager, the eldest, Fleetwood, was the heir apparent and would have held a position of esteem with the rest of the family. Fleetwood's early and sudden death thrust Peter into the limelight, a position that he probably did not relish at all. The 3rd brother, Peers, developed into a very capable man indeed, running the estates in the 1740s during the infirmity of their uncle. After the death of Peter Legh the Elder he managed the Bank Hall estate and later had some success as a merchant based at Liverpool. The youngest brother, Ashburnham, took holy orders and became Vicar of Davenham, Cheshire, from 1745-1775. He resided at Golborne Park, a fine estate on Rob Lane, north of Newton. Although he was a vicar, he spent the latter part of his life running the Golborne estate for his brother Peter, probably using curates at Davenham.

The handwriting styles of the four brothers give an indication of their personalities. Fleetwood's was neat and precise, Peers' was flowing and sure, Ashburnham's fast and confident. However, Peter's handwriting never developed from his childhood. It gave the impression that he suffered from some form of affliction, as it staggered across the page.

The two brothers, Peers and Ashburnham, corresponded often with Peter, relating private and business news interspaced with gossip. The feelings that the three brothers had for each other is evident in their letters. Below is Peers writing to his brother Peter in 1743:-

"Your kind letter I received per your servant, in which are so good to mention any Confinement in being here; do assure you Brother its far from that, but pleasure to serve so good a friend as you have been to me which I shall ever Acknowledge."

And in another letter about a future employee:-

"This comes by Thomas Lowes Son, who had been with you as this day, Could not get him a horse. Doubt not but the Young man will Answer haveing the Carrector of being both Sober and Industrious."

In 1747 Peers wrote concerning Herbert Yoxall the cartographer:-

"Yesterday I received yours and rejoice with you; hope Sister Legh and
the little one are harty. Last Thursday I was at Haydock were Mr
Tomlinson gave me the meeting, sent for Yoxall who acknowledged the
over charge of Acre's in the surveying, I was surprised when you sent me
Mr Tomlinson Account he tells me he'l finish his Maping as soon as
Possible then I will make the Deductions of his over charge."

At that time, Herbert Yoxall was living in Newton, possibly at the
BYH house in Rob Lane. The house referred to had the letters B, Y and
H built into it forming a triangle. The initials reputedly standing for his
name: Bernard Herbert Yoxall. He had been commissioned by Peter
Legh to survey and draw two maps of the Haydock and Newton
townships. The letter gives the impression that Peers had caught him
overcharging. Peers Legh never married and died in 1774 while he was in
residence at Bank, aged 60.

Peter's other brother, Ashburnham Legh, was a different character
altogether, having an air of flamboyance and eccentricity about him, even
though he was a man of the cloth. His letters have a lighthearted
whimsical feeling to them, even when he was relating mundane events.
Below he was informing Peter about a building project at Golborne Park:-

"On Wednesday last honest Ralpho and I met, talk'd over our design and
took a View the next Morn, to which I invited Your other able Counsellor
Shaw Ellinson whose little sketch, clear and sound Parts, made me quit
happy; This week we begin to cast our Clay, and have entirely left the
whole to their much better Management. On Friday Shaw is to be with
me, and hope by Saturday's Post to send you up our design which will be
executed within the Time we talk'd of; The Situation, I assure you far
exceeded my Expectation, which makes us doubly happy and unspeakably
thankful. To this and all others let me not forget to add our very sincere
Thanks for Your charming Present of a Side of Beef finer and better was
never tasted. We are greatly afraid Your Journey to Town wou'd prove

very uncomfortable, One hopes that you are all well will give real
pleasure to those who join in very sincere Affections. "

The two men he referred to in the letter were agents of Peter Legh:
Ralph Leigh and Shaw Allanson. The term "honest Ralpho" was very apt
because he was known as a strict and upright person.

In the next letter he was waiting with anticipation for his Master, a
term he used for his Brother, Peter.

"I expect my Master every Hour, who intends to take up his Quarters here
Tonight; Can't say I ever was more desirous of his coming in my Time
that we might drink our Friends in Greek Street in Your noble Cocoa over
Your right double Colchester which I expect every Min; so far I had
wrote last Night, and am now at 2 o'clock Saturday Afternoon in my
Chair in Expectation of my Worthy Friend."

Greek Street, Soho, London, was where Peter Legh stayed when
he was at Parliament. Ashburnham's affection for his brother, Peers, is
shown in the extract below:-

"I never was so much in Love with Peers as at this Time, cou'd I but see
Him here, I'd lick the Rogue's brown Face as white as Snow, I have an
uncommon Desire to see Him."

The reference to Peers' brown face confirms his employment as a
sea merchant and his face would have stood out among other gentry.
Ashburnham Legh died in 1775, at the age of 59. His greatest claim to
fame was that he was the father of Thomas Peter Legh, Lord of Lyme
from 1792-95.

Peter Legh the Younger was very lucky in having two brothers as
industrious and caring as Peers and Ashburnham. Throughout their adult
life they assisted him with the many estates and interests that the family
possessed. The three brothers were very close, even though Peter was
acknowledged as Master and Lord of Lyme.

Sisters

Peter Legh the Younger had five sisters, Elizabeth, Margaret, Ann, Sarah and Mary. Only one of them married. Elizabeth became the wife of the Rev. John Holt of Hartlebury in Worcestershire. Most of the others became independent of the family at Lyme, living off the money provided by the 1723 agreement. One of the sisters, Sarah, lived in Liverpool in average to poor circumstances. She died in 1762 and her funeral is described in detail by Ralph Leigh, Peter's agent at Haydock. He had organised the funeral, which no member of the family attended, and reported to Peter Legh:-

"These serve to advise you with the death of Your sister Sarah who was interrd the 19th Inst at St Georges Church in Liverpool in the following manner -- viz an exceeding good coffin and burying sheete -- carried to church by 6 common men Apiece and six bearers with each a wt (white) Hatt band tied with Black Ribbond and gloves 2 clergy men and Doctor Parr with each Hatt band and gloves, Clerk and Sextons with Hatt band and gloves -- 2 mormons followed the corps with each a crape hatt band and gloves and white and red port wine at the house for such as choose to take of it which method I hope will not be disagreeable -- I paid all her debts of every kind as farr as I co'd informe my self which I imagine was the whole which is as Under with the cash by her which I admire I met with any as the person she boarded with I take to be a [Trim]-- She expected I sho'd have left her all her close etc but to her disapointment I took all away that night after she was interred In which I hpoe you'l judge I was right we box'd 'em up and I expect 'em at Haydock tomorrow by 11 o'clock after which they shall all be put in good order for your sister to dispose of as she sees good (Who I imagine must have the disposal of 'em)"

Of all the sisters of Peter Legh the Younger, it was Ann that had the greatest influence. She was the one that stayed at home and controlled the everyday running of his life, becoming the mistress of Lyme. As the years passed Ann's power in the household grew. She became a virtual tyrant by the end of his life. The previous letter shows that as early as 1762 she had to be consulted over a small detail such as clothing. Peter's increasing ill health, due to hereditary problems and poor diet, aided Ann, allowing her to isolate him from outside influences. His weak will and shallow character were notorious and she was able to dominate him and the household totally. Servants, tenants and friends alike were very wary of her as she stalked the passageways of Lyme, inquisitive and ever critical, always to be avoided.

By the 1780s, Ann's control of the Lyme staff was complete. She insisted on vetting all new servants, who were immediately dismissed if they did not suit. One case highlighted this in 1790, when a friend of Richard Orford wrote with an apology:-

"I am sorry my sister was not successful at Lyme, I have reason to think she had to overcome a person that has too much influence with Mrs A. Legh."

Her correspondence with Richard Orford gives an indication of her character and the strength of her personality:-

"Your Bills came safe to Hand, but I must Desire not to be long before you send me more money for I have a grate want of it at present, ----- let me have all the news you know in all parts,"

"I must Desire you to send me a Hundred Pound by the 20 of May for I have many Bills for to pay and I shall be much obliged to you if you co'ld spair me fifty more, Direct for me at Bath."

"I want for to hear from you how your last day at Haydock was, with regard to that Affair of Molly, but do not name this to any Body in town,"

"I expect my Brother to night, as to that affair of Molly's I wonder at nothing all tho I have no thing to do with it, you have don the best you co'ld for your master and I do sincerely beleive you allways will, did you hear any thing of French when you was in town, the place she went into after mine the Lady cept her but won fortnight she was so Dredfull a Drunkard."

*"I find I can't do with less then fifty pound: so if you'll be so good to send
me Drafts for so much I shall think my self much obliged to you, I must
just tell you I never had upon the road so many Bad things happen to me
of expence my Chais was 3 times Broak down which you must think has
cost me a dell but do not name it to my Brother poor man for I shall not."*

The intrigues of upstairs-downstairs politics are evident in the
letters and there was a certain amount of collusion between Ann Legh and
Richard Orford. It is also evident that Orford held most of the purse
strings, confirming the idea that the two people completely controlled
Peter's life in the 1780s.

Further confirmation of Ann's power is contained in a deposition
made in the 1790s by Ellen Hancock, a former servant at Lyme Hall.
Ellen had worked as lady's maid to Mrs Legh for seven years before 1778
and had then returned as housekeeper in 1790. She had then held that
post until two months before Peter's death in 1792.

The document is quite rare for its time, thoughts of servants
concerning their masters are seldom recorded. Depositions are evidence
given by individuals in a court, in this case, possibly because Peter's Will
was being contested.

Ellen Hancock testified:-

*"That during the whole period of her former service to Mrs Legh wife of
the said Peter Legh and Ann Legh his sister resided with him. That when
she came to live as Housekeeper in the year 1790 as before stated Mrs
Legh was dead and Mrs Ann Legh his sister resided with and continued to
reside with him during the time this disposition was there."*

The extent of Ann Legh's control over the Legh household
appeared in the next statement:-

*"That as she this Dept. apprehends and believes Mrs Legh had no
influence or control over Mr Legh her husbands affairs or concerns but
the said Mrs Ann Legh his sister had considerable Influence or Control."*

Next, there was a statement concerning the relationship between the sisters-in-law:-

"That during the time of this Dispts. first residence at Lyme the conduct and behaviuor of the said Mrs Legh his wife was much more and kind and affectionate when the said Mrs Ann Legh was occasionally absent from Lyme then when she was there."

This indicates that Martha Legh had a pleasant personality, but her attitude to staff was influenced by her strict sister-in-law. By the 1790s Ann had totally cut Peter off from the outside world, business as well as personal. Ellen Hancock's testimony continued:-

"Saith that in general no personas were permitted to see Mr Legh until they had seen Mrs Ann Legh and even his steward Mr Orford, as well, during the Dept's first residence as her second residence at Lyme generally saw and consulted Mrs Ann Legh before he did business with her brother and that if any Tenants or other had favours to request from Mr Legh they thought themslves sure of obtaining what they wanted if they had got the consent of Mrs Ann Legh as this Dept. had observed and heard as she verily believes."

It is obvious that even Richard Orford, the most powerful of Peter's servants, had to tread lightly and bow to the greater influence of Ann Legh. She had become a dictator over all his family, friends and tenants alike. Another contemporary reference to Ann came in the letters of Thomas Davenport. He calls her "The Abbess", a term that denotes strictness and severity. Poor Peter, completely dominated, meekly acquiesced to all of her demands during the last years of his life.

Will

Peter Legh signed his will on 9th October 1787, five years before his death. The fact that he had not produced a male heir to whom he could pass on his many estates, must, in some way, have been a great disappointment to him. It is clear, from the will, that Peter's prime objective was to provide money for his daughters and their families, and the document went into great detail upon that point. The heir to the estates was mentioned in the briefest of terms, in 1787 it was his nephew, Thomas Peter Legh. He was referred to by the remark: "to the person in possession of my Capital Messuage called Lyme Hall". However, his daughters, two of whom were executrixes of his will, were referred to continually throughout the document.

The will was divided into five main parts and began with a will's normal rhetoric, committing his body to the earth and the settling of all of his debts.

In part one, Peter Legh instructed three men: Legh Master, the Rev. Legh Hoskin Master and Richard Orford, to hold certain properties in Dalton, Newton, Golborne, Disley and Broad Hinton, in Wiltshire, upon trust, to sell for the best price and collect rents to be paid to his executrixes. All the resulting money was to be applied to the payment of his debts, funeral expenses and legacies. It is worth noting that the three men he picked for that task were two cousins, one of whom was in America, plus a trusted servant.

Part two referred to the binding agreements of 1723 and 1737 regarding the intended marriages: Fleetwood Legh to Merial Leicester and Peter Legh to Martha Benet respectively.

Throughout the will there were repeated references to those agreements, and they were to control the livelihood of the Legh family during that century and even beyond. The first agreement, dated 23rd November 1723, was made between Peter Legh the Elder and various other parties, to settle all his lands, estates and buildings in male tail upon his nephew, Fleetwood Legh. The agreement began with the settlement of the estates upon Fleetwood Legh, in consideration of the intended marriage with Meriel Leicester, the daughter of Sir Francis Leicester. It then provided the sum of £4000 to be raised from the sale or rent of several estates for the younger brothers and sisters of Fleetwood Legh. The 1723 agreement was reaffirmed on the 20th December 1737, nominating Peter Legh the Younger as the heir to the estates, but retaining the same stipulations. On the whole the agreements are very complicated, with the majority of the estates being signed over to a third party, before reverting back to the family after the death of Peter Legh the Elder.

Part three listed all his daughter's children and made further provision for them. It confirmed the £10,000 mentioned in the 1737 agreement and added a further £10,000 to be divided equally among them.

Part four was specifically about the Bank Hall estate in Bretherton and Tarlton. The estate was to be used by Legh Master and then to be passed down to George Anthony Keck. If no issue resulted from George Keck, the estate was passed down in precedence to other members of Peter's immediate family.

Part five wrapped up all of the loose ends in the following way:-

"I Will that all my library of books, statues, pictures, furniture etc in Lyme Hall and Haydock Lodge shall go along with the Mansions as Heirlooms."
"I bequeath all red and fallow deer, persian sheep and wild cattle at Lyme and all fire engines, coal pit gear etc in use at my coal works to the person first in possession of my Capital Messuage called Lyme Hall after my decease, upon condition that he confirms the leases made on the settled estates."
"All goods, rent arrears, stocks of coals and all clear money which shall arise from the sale of all the manors, messuages and lands after the payment of my debts, funeral expenses, legacies and charges. I Will the same to be divided between my daughters and the children of my daughter Henrietta Atherton."

Between the date of Peter's will and his death, two codicils were added, one in August 1789 and a second in May 1791. The first codicil was quite normal and necessary, due to the death of one of his immediate family. Peter's youngest daughter, Hester, had died in 1789 and his granddaughter, Henrietta Maria, had come into considerable wealth, so a re-arranging of money was to be made. The personal effects and extra money that had been left to Hester Legh were to be passed down to his sister, Ann. The final part of the first codicil stated that his daughter, Elizabeth Keck, was to be the sole executrix.

However, the second codicil, added only 12 months before his death, was more important and in all probability caused more problems. It revoked completely part 4 of the original will and passed down to his sister, Ann, all the estates in Bretherton and Tarleton. Such a major alteration to his will, done shortly before his death, must have caused repercussions with other members of the family, especially persons that would have gained in the original will.

Peter Legh's will must have been contested soon after his death. The fact that Ellen Hancock's deposition exists points to somebody questioning the sanity of Peter in his last days, and questioning whether he had been coerced into making alterations. In all probability it was the Lilfords and George Anthony Legh Keck who made an appeal against the second codicil. They later gained control of the Bretheton and Tarleton estates and Ann Legh was to die in poverty a few years later.

Servants

In the eighteenth century large country houses, such as Lyme, were the largest employers of labour from their locality. Lyme Park would have abounded with Stewards, Gamekeepers, Gardeners, Grooms, Housekeepers, Maids, Footmen and the like. The majority of staff at Lyme were drawn from families in the local area, ie: Disley, High Lane and Pott Shrigley.

Besides the big divide between what was later termed upstairs and downstairs, there were internal levels that were strickly adhered to within the servants' hierarchy. Higher levels of staff such as Stewards, Agents etc. would congregate and socialise together, without lower ranks being present. They protected their hard won position in the household and woe betide anybody who attempted any intrusion. At Lyme they met in the Stone Parlour, a room that was used for daytime meetings and evening get-togethers. Peter Legh's Haydock Agent, Samuel Rigby, referred to it many times in his letters in the following way:-

"pray my compliments to the ladys and gentlemen of the Stone Parlor"

There were strict rules with regard to servants' behaviour, cleanliness and dress, especially those in contact with the owners.

Staff that came in close contact with members of the family, ie. personal maids etc., were usually brought from far afield - the further the better. Welsh, Scottish, Irish and even foreign servants were preferred, because they created less gossip in the district, being looked on as outsiders by the locals and becoming part of their own clique or set. Wages of such staff were low and very rarely increased during their employment. This is a letter from Ann Legh, the sister of Peter Legh the Younger, to Richard Orford in 1779, about the behaviour of her personal maid:-

"As I have discharged my Servant Mary Moseley I think it proper you
should know that I have pay'd her all that is due to her which when I
come to Lyme I will give you, receipted by Mary Moseley, I have hired

another Servant who came to me the 14th of September her Wages 9
Guineas a year, to be pay'd every year or per year. I gave Mary Mossley
a frank directed to you in which I told her to write to you to desire Her
Box might be sent direct'd, where she would send you word by Pickford's
Waggon, which I shall be much obliged to you to do."

Any form of misdemeanour was immediately stamped on, with
the threat of dismissal or loss of privileges hanging over the perpetrator.
An example of this was the letter from Hester Legh to Richard Orford in
1775:-

"My Mamma desires you to tell Dick Ryle that she
Demands that Guinea and half which he received from her as an
encouragement to behave well, but as his behaviour was more drunk'or
and abusesive afterwards she give's him as peremptory Orders to return
the money into your hands as he did Richard Major to return his Coat,
she desires you will write by return of Post to say that you have The
Money. My Mamma insists upon Dick Ryle not Dineing in the Stone
Parlour but to continue in the same situation as when there was an upper
Cook, for he cannot bear the least raiseing."

Some sympathy must be given to Dick Ryle, the money probably
instigated further trips to the local inns. However, the letter showed what
a privilege access to the Stone Parlour was.

Pleasantries between the owner's family and staff were kept to a
minimum. It was essential that servants knew and were kept in their
place and, as in the present day, the hardest taskmasters were those raised
to a higher position in life, fearful of a return to the ranks.

From the point of view of the owner, the quality of his staff and
their performance was paramount, especially during visits by friends,
family and dignitaries. Any mistakes at that time, resulting in a loss of
face, brought shame on the house as a whole.

Servants of quality became well known in certain circles and
agencies were set up to advertise their expertise, as shown in a letter from
Messrs Riccard & Littlefear in 1777:-

"Ever since we Recd. your Favour of the 8th Inst. we have made it our business to enquire for a Butler and have this Day had one Recommended to us. His name is John Taylor, lived with Mr Shuttleworth Member for Lancashire, (where he supposes you had some Knowledge of him) but last with Lord Donegal he seem'd desirous of knowing your Terms, of which we could not inform him, but enquiring his, he hintes at 30 Guineas a Year. He is a good looking person seems to Answer your Description, says he can be well Recommended, and will hold himself disengaged for your Answer, We shall be always happy to render ourselves serviceable to you in this or upon any other Occasion."

The letter from the agency shows just how staff moved around the country. Peter Legh used the company, Riccard and Littlefear, a number of times and became friendly with their families.

Sometimes it was not all sweetness and light in the Lyme household, as can be seen when Martha Legh was having problems with the cook:-

"I cannot but acquaint you of the Cooks ill behaviour here for sometime past which I was wholly ignorant of till within this very little while; his Transactions of the day before he went has fully convinced me what turn he is of, He is very drunken and willfully so, and when he is drunk he is riotous and insolent, besides being very headstrong, therefore you ought to take care that he is withheld from drink as much as possible, and pray tell him from me I shall not soon forget his behaviour last Monday night, and that he must remember I have told him from his Masters Authority that he must be under the inspection of the Housekeeper, whoever she may be, that she must help to regulate the management of the Meat, and also in making his Bills of Fare; if his Pride will submit to these he may probably continue to be the Cook at Lyme; but if not, he shall have my hearty wishes and endeavours to be remov'd. Pray shew him this letter."

It is obvious that unruly and insolent staff caused terrible problems. Another example from the eighteenth century was the Steward, Worthington, who made the mistake of putting himself above certain members of the family:-

"Since I have Write this I'me tould of Worthington is gone to Bank and had not the Civility to Let me Know and enquire if I would have anything indeed he is the Most Sacey Impertinate servant that ever Was and far from a good One I'me sure Noe Master but his wo'd keep him I was lately tould how Abominable Rude he is that when he speaks of my Nephew Legh hee Calls him Fleetwood Legh and the Rest: all by there Xtian Names without Master or Miss joyned to it: as Molly and Sally etc: and the same time his Bratts Must be Master and Miss Worthington Ive really noe patience hee grows soe Rich and proud I only hope when hee has Rope enough hee'l hang Himself."

This letter was written by Frances Legh, the wife of Peter Legh the Elder. Her thoughts were repeated by other members of the Legh family about the proud Mr Worthington.

Sexual contact between landed families and members of staff certainly did occur quite often during the eighteenth century; a time with an easy-going attitude towards sex. The inevitable consequences of such contacts were hushed up and the young lady in question was given some form of gift. At Lyme it was sometimes a piece of furniture, which was passed down through the young woman's family with some pride. Evidence today indicates that certain Lyme chests of drawers have passed down through generations of local families. One amusing example of this type of behaviour appeared in 1760, in connection with Ashburnham Legh:-

"I declare I'd wash my Shirts before I would take another Servant MAID out of your friend Dick Davenport's family. I wish she had twins so as were born alive, that the justice might have one and the Old Gen. of Bank the other."

Other remarks on the subject indicate that the young lady in question was trying to claim from Ashburnham and this resulted in his cruel words on the subject.

Over-friendliness between staff was also discouraged, and the offending couple were ususally discharged. However, in some cases, the steward did plead their case:-

"Yesternight I discharged Kitty from Lyme, and immediately upon the receipt of Yours I sent for Young John Turner and interrogated him concerning her being with Child, who said this morning (and not before) She told him She believed She was with Child. I then told him what I fear'd would be his fate; at which he was ready to drop down, I am very sorry for him: he being Lame is very unfit for other kinds of busyness. It would be exceed Charitable, if you are determined to part with him (even for the tender respect you always show to his Father) to recomend him to some other Gent."

Some members of staff acquired, over a number of years, a position of trust and privilege. Also there was a certain amount of prestige in having quality and faithful staff. Erddig, in North Wales, became famous for its servants and servants' hall. However, most large houses had their quota of characters and Lyme was no exception. During Peter Legh the Younger's time Lyme was blessed with such notables as: Richard Orford, who became a power unto himself, being in control of all his master's monetary dealings; Joseph Watson, the most famous of Lyme's servants, with his gallon of beer a day and expertise in deer management; James Grimshaw, the agricultural agent at Haydock, whose letters were full of comical asides and 'don't tell I told you of this'; Samuel Rigby, the mining agent at Haydock, with his neat and particular accounting, whose detailed record of coal mining still exists today and the villainous John Serjeant, the engineer, with his intrigues and bad practices, who finally suffered the wrath of his master.

On the whole, a servant's life at a large country house was full of hard toil, menial tasks and long days. For female staff marriage was the only form of escape; an escape not to an easier life, but at least to a more independent one.

𝔙𝔦𝔠𝔱𝔲𝔞𝔩𝔰

A large house such as Lyme, like most other country houses in the eighteenth century, would have been at the centre of a network of supplies. Produce of all types was transported from all parts of the country, primarily from their own estates, but from other sources as well. Lyme itself was known for the quality of its venison, and many letters in the family correspondence refer to Peter distributing it around the country. An example of the venison trade is shown below, when Peers Legh sends Peter a list:-

> *"Wo'd you please to have Venison sent to all the Gentlemen whose names are underwritten - if not to all, to which of them,*
> *Mr. Culcheth of Culcheth*
> *Mr. Richmond of Grange*
> *Mr. Banks of Winstanly*
> *Mr. Hanley Rector of Winwick*
> *Richard Brook of Norton*
> *Mr. Thornicroft of Thornicroft*
> *Mr. Blackburne of Orford*
> *Mr. Vaudrey of Warrington"*

Haydock and Newton were known for vegetables such as potatoes, beans etc. and a certain acreage of wheat and oats were also grown. The man in charge of agriculture at Haydock in the 1770s and 1780s was James Grimshaw, one of Peter Legh's agents. His letters were full of remarks about other people and his boss, Richard Orford. Below are some sections from his letters to Richard Orford. They give a clear picture of farming life and show the type of food that the Leghs and possibly their servants were eating:-

> *"that Day you left Haydock your Brother came and I sould him the fat Cow for 10£ 15shillings what is give back is left to me; we have finished planting Cabbage and soed most part of the Turnip;"*

> *"Yesterday we got in about the half of our Oats, would have got in the remainder but it has rained all this Day, shall now go on with Cutting the*

Wheat as fast as the weather will permit, should be glad to see you at Haydock but not with an Empty Pocket. "

The majority of the letters written by James Grimshaw about that time, were using the free post of Robert Gwillym. His last remark was referring to being without money to pay the bills.

"I had a letter from Mr Legh wherein he Enquired about the Young Turkeys and when I answered they was all right but last Saturday Night we Judg that a fox came and took away 5 of the Young Turkeys so that there is but 4 left;"

In the last extract, it sounds as if James could be in for a spot of bother from his Master, but all went well and he survived for many years to come.

"We have finished Shearing all but a part of the Beans."

"You have sent no Hops we shall miss this fine bruing weather,"

"No Mushrooms this year. I can assist you with Onions and Celery but no Cucumbers."

These letters show that the supplies were well organised and people were living off a varied diet. To transport all the produce a wagon ran from Lyme to Haydock and back again once a week:-

"I received yours, and will meet your Waggon as usual on Saturday the 7th of Feby with Potatoes."

The weekly wagon was referred to many times in the Legh correspondence and must have been an essential part of the running of the food supplies and other goods.

During his visits to London, Peter would report to his steward any cheap goods that he could find in the markets:-

"All sorts of Flesh Meat are cheap here Except Veal, But Oats that I laid in last year at 11 Shillings a Quarter are now 18 so that Ive good Interest for My money."

Lyme Park, in Peter's time, was well known for its entertaining and the quality of its hospitality. A dinner menu for 1778 gives an indication of the type and amount of food consumed on those occasions:-

Soup

Snipe Pie   Rabbits with Onions

Epurgne

Loin of Venison   Rague of Veal

Boild Mutton

Rost

Fillet de veau   Mince Pies

Woodcocks

Rst

Blance   Jelly

mange   Epurgne

Brokely   Giget de Gibeire

Turkey

Rst

Lady Newton, in 'The House of Lyme', made the comment that the table must have been groaning under the weight of all the food because it was customary to bring all the dishes at once.

The 19th century diary of the Whittington family refers to the amount of food that was consumed in Peter's time at Lyme:-

"In old Mr. Peter Leghs days the consumption of veal only for 5 months at a time during his residence at Lyme cost £150 a month - 3,000 fowls were used in the year - 12 packs of flour in a month and 500 pounds of butter per month."

If some of the figures are reduced to a weekly level they become: 57 birds, 3 packs of flour and 125 pounds of butter.

Drink, such as wines, spirits, ales and ciders, was an essential part of eighteenth century life. Alcoholic drink was brought from all parts of the country and even abroad. The next letter is by Peter Legh the Younger to his steward:-

"As I've a Hogshead of French Wine now at Leverpoole (at Mr Whalys) which I intend for Lyme, the same Cart that brings Up that may also bring up the Hogshead of Port you purchased of Gerrard Leghs, which you may adjust when you go to Heydock in February, but observe to order A Couple of fresh Iron Hoops to be put upon the French Hogshead before its put into the Cart."

The French wine referred to must have been quite costly since Peter gave instructions for its extra protection.

Another reference to the wagon appeared in 1788, when James Grimshaw was transporting rum:-

"I received a letter from you saying you had ordered a 20 or 25 Gallon Cask of Rum to be got ready to come by the Waggon."

The foreign spirits, such as rum and brandy, came in by Liverpool, the biggest local port. The Legh family would have had a regular dealer in the town. James Grimshaw reported his bill-paying trip in 1789:-

"I think I did not mention to you my Liverpool journey. I paid Mr Newsham his Bill £148-12s-6d and Mr Lawson for Rum and Brandy £20-7s-6d."

A rare reference to cider appeared in 1778, in a letter from Benjamin Arrowsmith of Upton upon Severn:-

"Yours duly came to hand, You may rely upon having two Casks of the best Cyder sent you, that our plantations can produce - but should by no means advise you to have it forwarded at present, being a very improper Season for moving that Liquor - The Time we always forward those Goods is the Months of February and March, and if agreeable to you,

shall send yours at that Time. You may have it sent either to Liverpoole, Warrington or Manchester, which one is most convenient to you, and if you have any Friend, at any of those Places, who would take Care of them, should be oblig'd to you for his adress, as having it lodg'd in common Warehouses, is frequently subject to have the Liquor damag'd. If you or your Friends should have occasion at any Time of Cyder or Perry in Town, should be happy to serve you there, having open'd Warehouses in the Adelphi. Have got some remarkable fine curious Perry more by me in Bottles, upwards of three years old, very Rich and High in Flavour."

There is a possibilty that Peter acquired the taste for cider during his many trips to Bath and the surrounding area.

In the capable hands of Peter Legh and his steward, Richard Orford, Lyme became known for good food, drink and hospitality, but in all probability this reputation faded towards the end of Peter's life. Peter's ill health must have taken its toll and caused him to retire from the partying scene.

𝔐𝔓

Newton in Makerfield was for many years one of the fortunate boroughs that were allowed to return two Members of Parliament, even though its population was small when compared to an area like Manchester. It was often referred to as a pocket or rotten borough, because the selection of its MPs was always in the hands of the largest landowner which, in the eighteenth century, was the Legh family. They had gained control of the township of Newton in 1660 when Richard Legh purchased the manor, borough and barony from the Fleetwood family for £3,500.

Before 1620 the Lord of the Manor was allowed to select the members for his borough. But after that date selection was entrusted to the local burgesses, or people owning freehold property of a certain value. However, in practice, it still lay with the Lord due to his power and influence over the local landlords. A selection of the eighteenth century MPs for Newton shows how influential the family name could be:-

Thomas Legh -- Peter Legh the Elder's brother.
John Ward   -- Peter Legh the Elder's lawyer.
Sir Francis Leicester - Fleetwood Legh's father-in-law.
Legh Master -- Peter Legh the Younger's cousin.
Peter Legh the Younger himself.
Anthony Keck -- Peter Legh the Younger's son-in-law.
Robert Gwyllim -- Peter Legh the Younger's son-in-law.
Thos. Peter Legh -- Peter Legh the Younger's nephew.

If any person aspired to parliament they would make an abject request to the then Lord of Lyme:-

"Sir,
Upon the rumour that Parliament was going to be dissolved I took the liberty of sending you by letter My desires of becoming one of the representatives of the borough of Newton -- by your silence I am to conclude that the contents of My letter displeased you or that some other

reason prevented your answering it -- Although I certainly asked a favor in requesting your support -- yet as there was not an absolute necessity of your complying I could not have been reasonably displeased or disappointed at being refused under your hand. I imagine that Sir Thos Davenport desires no interest in his Election from family connection with you -- nor from any property in the borough nor any acquaintance with the voters -- Upon the latter recommendations I could venture to try my own Interest against his -- and I believe upon an Explanation I could have merited an Equal share of your attention -- thus I proceeded from any alarm that My pretensions may have occasioned -- then I can also set you at ease -- At present the honour of representing Newton is the object of My own Wishes -- but had I (vice versa) been the object of their choice I should have thought myself bound to find out and support their real and true right of Election which at present seems doubtfull. Then indeed I could not reasonably expect a correspondence with you at present I flatter Myself that I have done nothing to forfeit the acquaintance which I hoped had commenced when I was last in Lancashire."

The writer of this plea was a Mr. William Brown Brotherton of Harley St., London. It was one of the better class requests, intelligently and persistently put, in a clear and confident hand. Apparently his request was refused because his name does not appear in the list of Newton members.

Today, it would be looked on as a rather corrupt way of conducting an election, but it was very favourable to the Lord, who required men of his own point of view in positions of power. By the end of the 18th century things had begun to change, as many people demanded freedom of selection. Circulars and news-sheets began to appear in Newton demanding change, but it wasn't until 1831 that the pocket or rotten boroughs disappeared.

Peter Legh the Younger's parliamentary career began in 1743 and he represented Newton until 1774. Information from the House of Commons shows that he was a conscientious MP, regularly attending and voting on various bills. The Duke of Newcastle, Prime Minister in the 1750s, looked on him as a 'sure friend' in Parliament. Poor health was probably the reason for him giving up his seat in 1774, when he put one of his nephews in at Newton. A letter written by Robert Gwillym thanks Peter for his kind offer:-

"I accept your kind offer with Pleasure and great Thankfullness; not that I propose to myself any Emolument or much Satisfaction by being in Parliament, but I think it makes one of more Consequence in the Country where one lives, I should be glad therefore to be in one Parliament which I dare say will give me enough, only let me hope that it is not your Regard for me, but your own Inclination that induces you to decline serving any longer, as I assure you it will give me the most sincere Pleasure at all Times and in all Places to prove myself your ever dutyfull & affectionate Servant.

R.V.A. Gwillym.

Mrs: Gwillym & little Elizabeth continue as well as their Friends can desire. Our affec. Regards attend all at Lyme".

Robert Gwillym did not attend Parliament often because he suffered from bad health.

In the eighteenth century, Parliament was thronged with famous men; men that are still remembered in the present day. Sir Robert Walpole is still known as our first Prime Minister. Others were the Duke of Newcastle, the Earl of Chatham, known as Pitt the Elder, Lord North and Pitt the Younger, who became Prime Minister in his twenties. Peter Legh may have been in contact with them, but it is highly probable that he made little impression on them.

𝕿𝖗𝖆𝖉𝖊

In the eighteenth century, a majority of the local landowners took part in trade in some form or other. Products from estates were bartered or traded over great distances throughout the country. The Lancashire estates of the Legh family provided agricultural produce for staff, family and trade alike. Some landowners developed natural products from their estates, such as timber, clay and sand.

The more fortunate landowners discovered on their lands minerals which provided great wealth and security for many years. In the case of the Legh family it was coal that provided the wealth for the future.

From the seventeenth century onwards, coal was required in ever increasing amounts to fuel the industrial revolution that was sweeping the country. Commercial coal mining, with the north east in the forefront, was becoming commonplace throughout the nation, due to the profits that could be made by landowners and entrepreneurs alike.

In the vicinity of Lyme domestic coal mining was prevalent in the seventeenth century, but it was to be the Lancashire estates, centred around Haydock, that became the great asset for the Leghs.

During the time of Peter Legh the Elder coal had been mined to the north of Haydock. However, it became clear in the ensuing years that the seams that outcropped on the Gerard estates in Ashton ran southwards under Legh land. Lord Gerard's engineers may have developed the mines but at the border between the two estates it became Legh coal. The best of the seams found under Haydock were the Florida seams. They were named after the farm where they outcropped on the Gerard estates, but the majority of the coal lay under Haydock. Little did Peter Legh the Younger know in the early days what a great asset it was to be.

In the first half of the eighteenth century coal production was severly limited by the problems of transport. Because of this, coal mining in Haydock would have stayed within certain limits until the advent of the railway era. So the coal producers in the area derived most of their profit from local sales. However, in the 1750s, due to pressure from the salt proprietors of Liverpool, who needed coal in great quantities, a navigation or canal was cut that greatly improved the transport of coal from the Haydock district. The Sankey Navigation, as it became known, ran through Peter Legh's land for a great extent in Newton, Bradley and

C O A L S
To be SOLD by
W E I G H T,

Twenty Hundred to the Ton, and 120lb to the Hundred;

At the Proprietors Coal-Office, Opposite the *New Machine* on *Nova Scotia*, at the following Prices, *for Ready Money only:*

	Delivered to Flat-keepers, per Ton.			Delivered to Shiping per Tun.		
	£.	s.	d.	£.	s.	d.
Peter Leigh, Esq'rs Coal -	0	7	2	0	6	6
John Mackay, Esq'rs do. -	0	7	0	0	6	4
Thomas Case, Esq'rs do. -	0	6	10	0	6	2
Sir Thomas Gerrard's do. -	0	6	6	0	5	10

Any person taking a FLAT LOAD, may have any of the above said Coal, paying the Cost at the Pits, River Dues, Freight and Cartage. And to accomodate Poor Housekeepers, or such as cannot purchase a Ton at one Time, smaller Quantities will be delivered at the Yard, at *four pence halfpenny* per Hundred, of 120lb.

Sworn Agents will attend constantly at the said Coal-Office, to whom the Public may apply.

By Order of the Proprietors.

Sankey Navigation
Coal Delivery Advert.

Haydock. Its construction initially caused consternation to his agents, because of the damage it caused to their fields, but he soon realised what a great monetary benefit it was. Within ten years Peter Legh was transporting tens of thousands of tons of coal per year on the Sankey Canal. It had changed dramatically their coal works from a few holes in the ground to a thriving concern and changed the face of Haydock forever.

Throughout the 1740s and 1750s Peter Legh took great interest in his coal mines on the estates. He was, at that time, comparatively young and the novelty of being a coal producer probably amused him and his friends. However, from the 1760s onwards, he delegated most of the work, with all other estate responsibility, to his steward, Richard Orford. From 1760, till his death in 1790, Orford increased his control over most of Peter Legh's business dealings. He developed the coal mines, managed the estates, made most of the deals over land and coal contracts and became more respected than his master. When Richard Orford died in 1790, memorials were installed in churches at Disley, Prestbury and also at Winwick, where he was buried.

In the 1740s the Leghs were also involved in an immoral type of trade; transporting slaves to the West Indies. The letter shown below is typical of the time:-

"The (ships) Master writes he had got one hundred and ten fine slaves, his compliments about Three Hundred. we hope in God, he's got safe to Jamaica were he's to dispose of them, please God that he has not a great mortality, will do pretty well for us."

This letter was written in 1743 by Peers Legh to his brother, Peter, who at that time was living at Calveley. The way that the letter is worded indicates that Peter, also, was involved in their shipping.

In later years, trade, especially the coal trade, bore a certain amount of stigma and the Legh family tended to distance themselves from it. But it must be stated that all their future wealth, influence and power was on the whole provided by the black gold of Britain - Coal - mined in a little village in Lancashire - Haydock.

Era

What was Peter Legh's era like, and how did it fit into the stream of English history? Did Peter Legh and his immediate family make any impact on society? Or did they meander through their lives in an indulgent and extravagant manner. Peter's life almost covered the 18th century for he was born, raised, and he died within its limits.

England was ruled for most of the eighteenth century by three Georges, three kings who were known for entirely different reasons. George I was an indifferent, German speaking ruler, that left the running of the country to his ministers. George II was the last British king to lead his troops in battle. George III, who suffered from bouts of madness, lost the Americas.

Many terms have been attributed to the 18th Century -- a time of change, enlightenment, elegance, style, discovery and industry. The great changes which were occuring were in all levels of society and all aspects of life.

Visually, the style and elegance of the era appeared in the painting, furniture and architectural fields. Gainsborough and Hogarth, Chippendale, Hepplewhite and Sheraton, Robert Adam and Sir Robert Taylor altered the interiors and exteriors of English houses. Also great changes were made to the gardens of the gentry, with men like Capability Brown and Humphry Repton naturalising their surroundings.

From the end of the 17th century, a large number of country houses acquired a classical appearance. In the 1720s, Peter Legh the Elder, with the aid of his architect, Giacomo Leoni, greatly altered Lyme, but his nephew only carried out internal alterations. The work that Peter Legh the Elder did was funded by his coal mines in Haydock, as can been seen below:-

"I have been in these parts 10 days. I propose to stay another week and then return to my Masons I am raising money in these parts for them, and endeavouring to Amend your Coal pit road, tho I meet with some unexpected opposition."

Another reference appeared later in 1729:-

"I have had a tedious piece of work in a Foundation part of my New Building but hope I have secured it. My other Building goes on very well. I am forced to take the Derbyshire Aire for want of Room at Lyme."

After Peter Legh the Elder's labour of love, only slight changes were made to the house in that century. Lyme was radically altered in the 19th century by Wyatt and the house has kept its general appearance to the present day.

Technological progress during the eighteenth century was typified by the control and advancement of steam power. Primitive versions of steam engines were constructed during the first half of the century by Savery and Newcomen. But it was with the arrival of James Watt, the reluctant genius, that the steam engine was changed from an inefficient machine to a work-horse that changed the world.

Peter Legh the Younger became interested in steam engines, or fire engines as they were termed, in the late 1740s. Water problems in his Norbury coal mines caused him to install an engine to keep the workings clear. In the late 1740s Peter Legh the Younger was mining at Norbury in Cheshire, as well as at Haydock. In the next letter Peter is congratulating his agent on the work he had done concerning the engine:-

"You've done well in the consultation about the Fire Engine. And I very much incline towards it, and tho' its expensive I'l assuredly undertake it provided the quantity of coal to be got is likely to answer."

The steam engine did prove very successful, enabling them to reach deeper seams. Peter also installed an engine at Haydock a few years later. Fire engines became an essential tool for the eighteenth century coal owner, even though they were inefficient and required large amounts of fuel to run them.

Great changes also occured in transport and communication. Roads were poorly constructed and maintained during the first half of the century but, with the establishment of Turnpike Trusts, travel improved to a great extent. Weather always had a big influence on the condition of roads, with sometimes surprising results even in winter, as Peter related in 1748:-

"I had yours this Evening, have had the pleasantest Journey I ever had in my life, not a drop of Rain, Roads better than summer."

However, travel was sometimes very hazardous because of robbers and highwaymen. Peter Legh never mentioned the problem, but one of his MPs, Thomas Davenport, did refer to it in 1784:-

"My Colleague arrived yesterday, and was robbed near Finchley Common, turning out of the High Road there towards my house. He lost about 6 or 7 shillings, and his Servant about nine shillings, and the two Highwaymen damned him for not having so much Money as his Servant in a Laced Hat. Tom got out of the Chaise, & fired two Sluggs after his friends, but whether with effect or not he cannot tell."

In the above letter, Thomas Davenport was referring to Thomas Peter Legh, Peter Legh's nephew. Lack of security on most roads meant that this dramatic encounter with the highwaymen was typical of eighteenth century travel.

Postal services in the eighteenth century were always dependent on good roads and did improve during that time. Some complaints can be found in the Legh correspondence regarding delivery times. Below is Ashburnham Legh's amusing remark on the subject:-

"This Morn. I was favour'd with yours of the 14, which only makes it ten Day's in it passage."

Peter Legh was fortunate with the cost of his postage because he was an MP for many years. MPs and other government groups were allowed free postage for their personal correspondence. Sometimes this was disputed, as can be seen below in a letter from Thomas Lewis in 1761:-

"About Ten days ago, on the Receipt of Yrs I went to the General Post Office and shew'd your Letter to the Inspector of the Frank's -- he Cryed Peccavi, & said all thing's should be rectified for the Future - he wanted me to give him a List of the People's sent to, I told it would not be agreable to you to have your Privilidge limited,---------- Mr Saunders was

with me this morning to ask about the above, I told him what I had done,
which prevented his going on same errand -- I hope there will be no
charging for the Future and am Sr yr Faithful servant."

The free post 'perk' that Peter Legh had was often used by his
servants, such as Richard Orford, the Steward. Many letters in the Legh
correspondence are addressed to and from Peter Legh MP, but are in
reality internal letters between servants.

Without doubt, the most momentous event of the era was the loss
of the Americas in 1776. Bungling on both sides of the Atlantic spoiled
any relationship which existed between the two parties, and caused the
great rift that split the English speaking peoples for a hundred years. The
event shaped and produced the modern world and could have been
stopped with better diplomacy. The Leghs were involved because various
members of the family lived in the Americas. One of Peter Legh's
cousins, Legh Master jr., graphically described the general feeling in the
colonies in a letter written in August 1775:-

"I am informed the Ministry are determined to conquer the Americans. I
imagine they'll find it a much more difficult affair than they apprehend.
The Whole Continent are mustering and seem to be determined to die or
to conquer, for they are resolv'd never to submit to be taxt by parliament,
as to myself I must make all speed back that I may take my wife and
daughter to Providence that we may be out of the Way of mischief."

True and portentous words from Legh Master. For within twelve
months the declaration of independence was signed and the American
revolution had begun.

Peter Legh's era was also known for rioting and public disorder.
The many inventions of the age were causing the workers to be fearful of
losing their jobs. In the North it was the textile industry that took the
brunt of the mobs that were roaming the countryside. Below is a typical
example of that behaviour reported by James Grimshaw, the agent at
Haydock:-

"There has not been such Mobing this many Years as at this time there is
a Mob at this present time that is puling down all the Carding and

Spinning Machines that go by water, three is allready pull'd Down Mr
Unsworth is takeing his Down himself."

This type of behaviour was prevalent in many parts of the country and culminated in the Luddite riots of the nineteenth century.

Throughout the eighteenth century a general mixing and social intermingling had occured between the nobility and the landed gentry. The country became a social Utopia for the moneyed landed gentry, at places where similar people socialised, far removed from the poor and destitute. One of the places where the 'elite' congregated was Bath, the spa town. Bath became the 'in place' for the wealthy society person. The town was full of people enjoying parties, balls and the spa waters. It was Peter Legh's favourite place, where he met his future wife and where he spent most of his time during the season. There are many references in the family correspondence about his numerous visits to the premier spa town in the country.

To sum up the era of Peter Legh the Younger, or the eighteenth century as a whole, the elegance and visual style are the obvious attributes. However, underlying the beauty of the time, there was the harsh reality of the ordinary people. The poor and the disabled were ignored. Whores, libertines, gin shops, cock fighting, bear baiting and other cruel pastimes were commonplace. One of the nastier sides of eighteenth century life was graphically described by Elizabeth Keck in a letter written to her mother in 1768:-

"I suppose you have not (heard) of Lord Baltymore's late
transcaxtion, If I can I'll tell it you, there was 2 Miss Woodcocks sett up
in Millinery way, (by the by they were very handsome) there friends took
great pains to gett them into bussiness they had now sett up their
bussiness above a fortnight, when a jew and another Lady came into the
shop and bought a great quantity of things for which they paid ready,
after which the Lady turn'd to the prettier and told her to bring them
herself to a Mrs Hervey's who lived beyond the tower, which accordingly
the Girl did, where Lord B-- was ready to receive her, he importuned her
a great while but to no purpose (in short he almost Starved the Girl) one
night the jew said he was going to the play, upon which she beg'd the jew
to let her go with him that she might make her escape the jew consented;

and they got into a coach, where it drove directly to Lord B-- house in Bolton Row, there he importuned her again but all to no effect; upon that he immediately took her by force into the Country, there four men held her while My Lord had his wish, since that she has made her escape and has enter'd a prosecution against him and if my Lord does not go off he certainly will be hang'd, but what surprizes the world is that her Sister did not make a Strict search after her"

We can but wonder whether Lord Baltymore got his just deserts for the rape, or did he get off scot free?

The appearance and social attitudes of the century were dramatically portrayed by the works of William Hogarth, who became the conscience of the period, showing it with all its virtues and vices, in a series of thought provoking paintings and prints.

The Cock Pit by William Hogarth.

Mr Worthington

We have performed our journey to Stone with ye greatest Ease and pleasure, and I do verily believe Mrs Legh will almost be void of complaint before we reach London;

Pless ye Key of ye Library in ye Door which I'd have you send me up by ye first Box or parcell yt comes from Lyme, the King plest in ye Chair by ye Bed side will come safe in a Post Letter

I have altered my mind in reguard to the Bradley Wainscoat, and instead of ye drawing Room would have it put up in the Eating Parlour, And the Drawing Room fitted up in Plaister Panels as I before intended ye Other Room.

Write by ye return of ye post and your letter will meet me in Town

I am
Your very affe Master
PLegh

Stone
8th Decr 1748.

Letter by Peter Legh to his Steward.

70

Personality

How can Peter's personality be assessed in the present day? Family correspondence, be it misleading, misguided or downwright lies, is the finest contemporary source of information about a man's personality. Letters to and from Peter Legh the Younger give a clear insight into the many facets of his life: a shy young man, a settled married man, a doting father, a powerful landowner, a grieving father, a middle aged socialite and a dominated brother.

In his happily married days, Peter and Martha travelled the country together, be it to London, Bath or to other spas. The couple left the children at Lyme in the secure hands of trusted servants, but insisted on frequent reports of their progress. Peter's letters to those servants show his love for his children:-

"kiss our Dear Little Ones and tell Hen. Il send her Another Kiss in My next letter."

The Hen. referred to was Henrietta, his eldest daughter.

"I had yours this evening and with the utmost Joy to find our Dear Little ones so hearty and Merry, let nought be wanting to Keepe the Nursery Cheerful for I thinke My self under the Strongest Obligations to them for the Very Assiduous Care and Tenderness they have all shewed to our Dear Little Ones, you may depend upon hearing from Me punctually Every Post."

Peter Legh's appreciation of the good qualities of his servants was one of his great attributes.

"I had yours by the last post and rejoice to hear of the Nursery Mirth, and sh'ud not be very sorry to be within the hearing of it,"

"We rejoice to hear our Dear little Jewels are hearty and well, and whenever you leave home Order Thomas Marsland (as he's a tolerable Scribe) to write to Me every Post while you are away."

It can be seen that Peter required daily information on the children, but was not prepared to put up with bad handwriting.

The majority of Peter's correspondence at that time referred to his children, in some form or other. Throughout his life Peter was passionately involved in the welfare of his surviving children. Those that were married were financially supported and even after his death he ensured that they would want for nothing.

Another of Peter's attributes was that he was prepared to give references and assist people in bettering themselves. Two good examples are shown here:-

"A very deserveing young gentleman has applied to me for my Interest towards his obtaining Professorship of Moral Philosophy in the University of Oxford, as your friendship with Dr Hay of the Commons is I know great, His interesting in our Favour would have the greatest weight with Dr Fry Principle of St Johns College and in whose power the professorship is. The Young Gentlemans name is Barker, Fellow of Brasnose College and whose character is such as will make neither you nor me blush for such recomendation"

"I could not suffer this letter to go out of my hands with apologising for the trouble I give your Lordship. It is a Request to me from a very Ancient Tenant to gett his Son out of the Army. His name is Peter Lawson now quartered at Stamford in Lincolnshire in your Regiment and if your Lordship would be so good to give Him his discharge we finding another man it would be a great comfort to his aged parents who stand in great need of his assistance."

Peter sometimes took on the responsibility of a father figure to his servants, showing concern for their welfare. Below he was concerned about one of his maids being without support:-

"The best Jerimiah Swindells can do is to marry the Dairy Maid, which if he does not dismiss him (from) My service."

It is not known whether Jerimiah married the maid, who was probably with child. Although the above information shows Peter to be a kindly and benevolent master, he also required total loyalty from his staff, otherwise he could be ruthless, as can be seen below:-

"As to William Osbeson I think he has done very ill in letting his livery be made when his own intention was to quitt his Service however on the receipt of this discharge him, And if Hambletons Young fellow will learn to Shave and Buckle a Wigg I'l take him into my Service at My return into the Country."

The latter part of the letter indicates that the position in question was that of a personal servant. He would be dressed in full livery and would have attended Peter throughout the day.

Being Lord of Lyme, Peter was very concerned about the security of his estates. Problems with poachers and thieves were ever with Peter and his agents. His letters on that subject were always in the severest tones:-

"And I wish you may be able to find out the Villian, in Reguard to the Rascails that Infest the Game in Handley and the Sponds wherever you shall be able to catch them. take them before Mr Wright of Stockport (but Observe all Charges) are to be reimbursed by Mr Stafford who has Subscription money on that Amount. Order also Peter Wild to be very Watchful - And I desire No Persons whatever may be permitted to kill Any Game - nor shall I grudge any expence to find out this Denn of Thieves."

"As to roads through the Parke I know of None, So pull up all Stiles leading thereto at onst and proclaim it in Stockport and at all the neighbouring townships that neither foot or horse will be admitted to go through Lyme Park and order all the Park Gates to be shutt accordingly and at first watched."

These two letters were written in 1748 and 1763 respectively, showing the long term security problem that Peter Legh had with Lyme

Park. They also show how decisive he could be in his younger days. The 1763 letter was written to Richard Orford at the beginning of his stewardship, and the resulting notice was duly displayed in the locality.

As Peter Legh grew older, he suffered a series of mental and physical problems that totally re-shaped his attitude to life. His sad loss of his son, long term ill health, a tendency to hypochondria and hereditary problems coloured the rest of his life. Known for being a mournful, melancholic and weak-willed man, he became totally dominated by other people. Although a sad and ineffectual figure at the end, he had lived a full life. He has lately been misrepresented as the unknown Lord of Lyme, but he was not without many good attributes.

𝔇eath

Peter Legh the Younger, Lord of Lyme, died on 20th May 1792. He had been Lord of Lyme for over 48yrs and had not been well for a number of years. His old enemy, gout, had ravaged him throughout his life, and poor Peter was reduced to being wheeled around the Gallery at Lyme. Peter's problems with gout caused him to use rather extreme methods to alleviate the pain:-

"I wrote to Manchester about the Gout Chair and received for Answer the Inclosed from which I hope you will be able to find where the Chair and foot Cistern is gone."

The above mentioned chair and attachments sound more of an instrument of torture than anything else.

The Deposition of Ellen Hancock, previously mentioned, shows clearly what his last years were like:-

"in the year 1790 he was much afflicted with Gout and never left his bedroom but to be sometimes wheeled in a chaise along a gallery by a servant but she did not observe that his mind or understanding was impaired or less strong than it was when she formerly lived with him."

This indicates that he endured a lonely and sad end to his long and varied life, probably outliving most of his friends and associates. Peter's wife had died in 1787 and his famous servant, Richard Orford, just two years previously, in 1790. The only contact with the past was his sister, Ann, who outlived him by just a few years. He was buried at St. Mary's, Disley, setting a precedent for the majority of the future Lords of Lyme. No more would the mournful train toil its way from Lyme to Winwick with the sad load to be interred there. From that time onwards, all Lords of Lyme would be interred at St. Mary's, Disley. The only exception was Thomas Peter Legh, who, throughout his short life, resided in Newton and Haydock.

The only reminder in the present day of Peter Legh the Younger are his letters and the memorial tablet in St. Mary's, Disley, which reads as follows:-

Memorial Tablet at St. Mary's, Disley.

Sacred to the Memory of Peter Legh Esq
once the owner of Lyme Park
and all its large appendages
Reader learn hence the vanity of all earthly possessions
But emulate his bright example
In the cultivation of those virtues
Which enshrine him in the esteem and affection
Of his contemporaries here
And strengthened his hopes
Of a blessed immortality hereafter.
Through the merits of our redeemer.
Obit. May 20th. 1792. aetat 85.

Peter has completely disappeared from view, no visible grave and no portrait of him is known to exist. It is as if he and his memory have faded completely into the past. Although no painting has survived to the present day, some were done of him, because there are references in the correspondence:-

"I thought proper to inform you of my having in my hands 2 Pictures belonging to the late Countess Heywood of this place - the one your figure on Horseback in Crayons, large, and in an Elegant Gilt frame the Price is £2-2s."

It is possible that the above picture is the one that Lady Newton referrred to in 'The House of Lyme' as being at Lyme in 1917:-

"He wears a white wig and a three-cornered hat, a plain coat buttoned down the front, and a white "choker." There is little character in the face, which is weak and inexpressive."

It is obvious from these remarks that Peter was not glamorous enough for Lady Newton, with his long involvement in trade, industry and the nitty gritty of life. The many estates, buildings, coal works, cattle and other livestock, were passed down to his nephew, much to Peter's regret. An era of stability had come to an end for the Legh family and they

St. Mary's, Disley.

entered a period of uncertainty and change; a transitional period that carried on for many years until the middle of the nineteenth century. Many people, who were involved in that time of unrest, may have wished to return to the previous more stable period.

The last recorded thoughts of Peter Legh the Younger are in the 2nd codicil that was added to his Will in 1791. It is a touching, if misguided, tribute to his sister, Ann:-

"I bequeath to my dear sister Anne Legh all and every the sum and sums of money, plate, linen, china, goods and effects whatsoever which I am become intitled to as personal Representative of my said late daughter Hester Legh for her own use in consideration of her long and constant attendance upon me during the whole of my life and particularly during my present long and tedious confinement."

The last recorded reference about Peter Legh the Younger appeared after his death, showing some of his better attributes:-

"Old Mr. Peter Legh died May the 20th 1792 aged 85 his benevolent mind justly entitled him to rank amongst the best of men - his numerous tenants had to lament a mild and good landlord - his servants a kind and generous benefactor - his houses were for many years the few remaining examples of old English hospitality."

Bibliography and Sources

John Rylands University Library - Legh family collection - Correspondence.

Cheshire Record Office - Tabley collection - Correspondence.

Lancashire Record Office - Lilford Papers.

Lady Newton - The House of Lyme (1917).